my first
cookbook

Published by:
TRIDENT REFERENCE PUBLISHING
801 12th Avenue South, Suite 400
Naples, Fl 34102 USA

Tel: + 1 (239) 649-7077
www.tridentreference.com
email: sales@tridentreference.com

My First Cookbook
© TRIDENT REFERENCE PUBLISHING

Publisher
Simon St. John Bailey

Editor-in-chief
Susan Knightley

Prepress
Precision Prep & Press

Includes Index
ISBN 1582797277
UPC 6 15269 97277 9

Printed in The United States

introduction

Knowing how to cook is not only a skill for life, but can be great fun too. Being able to prepare even the simplest dish provides you with a great deal of satisfaction, and enables you to work towards being independent as you grow older. This book provides simple recipes that will help you prepare snacks, drinks and meals for yourself

or for the family. Use them to make sure you get the most enjoyment out of this activity, but don't forget there are some things you need to know before you start cooking.

10 Golden Rules for Success

- Always ask an adult such as your parents or an older brother or sister, if it is okay for you to cook. Also ask them to go through the recipe with you just in case you need help with some part of it. Ask if there is something you do not understand.

- First read the recipe from start to finish to make sure that you have all the ingredients and equipment that you will need. Ingredients are always listed in order of use so you can lay them out in that order.

- Always wear an apron. This will keep your clothes clean.

- If you have long hair tie it back, so that it does not get in the food or get caught in any equipment. Chefs and cooks wear hats for this reason.

- Wash your hands with soap and water before you start cooking. Remember to dry them well, as wet hands are slippery.

- Turn saucepans and frying pans so that the handles do not hang over the edge of the stove top.

- Take special care when plugging electrical appliances, using sharp knives and lighting the gas.

- Always use oven gloves when removing food from the oven or when handling hot saucepans or frying pans.

- Keep a clean damp cloth on hand to wipe up any spills as you go along.

- Always wash up when you have finished cooking. If something takes a while to cook this is a good time to do the washing up, otherwise do it after you have finished eating.

Difficulty scale

■□□ I Easy to do

■■□ I Requires attention

■■■ I Requires experience

scramblers

■□□ | Cooking time: 4 minutes - Preparation time: 5 minutes

method

1. Break eggs into bowl. Add milk and black pepper to taste. Whisk. Set aside.
2. Place butter in frying pan. Heat over a low heat until butter melts.
3. Add egg mixture. Cook until egg mixture is set but still creamy. Stir carefully from time to time.

....
Serves 4

ingredients

> **8 eggs**
> **2 tablespoons milk**
> **freshly ground black pepper**
> **30 g/1 oz butter**

junior chef says

Serve scramblers with hot toast. I like to cut a roll in half, toast it and then top with scramblers.

pancake
stacks

■□□ | Cooking time: 30 minutes - Preparation time: 5 minutes

ingredients

> 1 cup/125 g/4 oz
  self-raising flour
> 2 tablespoons sugar
> 1 egg
> 3/4 cup/185 ml/6 fl oz
  milk
> 30 g/1 oz butter

junior chef says

*Top pancakes with jam,
honey or golden or
maple syrup. Serve with
milk and muesli.
To make muesli, mix
10 chopped dried
apricots, 2 cups/185 g/
6 oz rolled oats,
1 cup/45 g/1 1/2 oz bran
flakes, 4 tablespoons
wheat germ,
4 tablespoons sultanas,
1/2 cup/45 g/1 1/2 oz
desiccated coconut
and 2 tablespoons
sesame seeds.*

method

1. Place flour in sifter or sieve. Sift into large mixing bowl. Add sugar.
2. Break egg into small bowl. Add milk. Whisk.
3. Make a well in center of flour mixture. Pour in egg mixture. Beat with wooden spoon until smooth.
4. Place a little butter in frying pan. Heat over a medium-high heat until butter melts and sizzles.
5. Pour 3-4 tablespoons of batter into pan (a). Cook until bubbles form on top of pancake (b). Turn over. Cook for 1-2 minutes or until second side is brown (c).
6. Place cooked pancake on plate. Repeat with remaining batter to make 10 pancakes.
7. Stack three or four pancakes on each serving plate. Eat pancakes with your favorite topping.

....
Makes 10

a

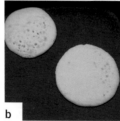

b

c

breakfast in bed

■ □ □ | Cooking time: 2 minutes - Preparation time: 20 minutes

method

1. To make juice, cut oranges in half. Place an orange half on squeezer. Twist to squeeze out as much juice as possible. Pour juice into glass. Repeat with remaining orange halves until you have a full glass of juice.
2. To make salad, remove green hull from strawberries. Cut strawberries in half. Peel fruit if necessary, chop, place in serving bowl. Top with strawberries. Spoon over yogurt. Drizzle with honey.
3. To make toast, place sugar and cinnamon in bowl or cup, mix. Place bread in toaster, toast until golden. Spread toast lightly with butter. Sprinkle with sugar mixture.
4. To make coffee, fill a microwave-safe mug with water. Heat on High (100%) for 1-2 minutes. Add instant coffee powder to water. Stir. Serve with or without milk and sugar.

ingredients

fresh orange juice
> 2-3 oranges

fruit salad with yogurt
> 4 strawberries
> 1-2 pieces fresh fruit of your choice
> 2 tablespoons natural yogurt
> 1 tablespoon honey

cinnamon toast
> 1 tablespoon sugar
> 1/4 teaspoon ground cinnamon
> 2 thick slices bread
> butter

a mug of coffee
> 1 cup/250 ml/8 fl oz water
> 1 teaspoon instant coffee powder

....
Serves 1

junior chef says

For fruit salad choose fruit that is in season. This has the best flavor and is the least expensive. In summer you could use peaches and apricots. In winter try apples and pears or bananas.

banana
smoothie

■☐☐ I Cooking time: 0 minute - Preparation time: 5 minutes

ingredients
> 1 banana
> 1/2 cup/125 ml/4 fl oz cold milk
> 1/2 cup/100 g/31/2 oz natural or fruit-flavored yogurt of your choice
> pinch ground nutmeg

method
1. Peel banana.
2. Place banana, milk and yogurt in food processor or blender. Process for 20-30 seconds or until thick and smooth.
3. Pour into glass. Sprinkle with nutmeg.

Makes 1

junior chef says

You can make smoothies using any fruit you like. How about trying one made with apricots, peaches or strawberries?

hot chocolate

■□□ I Cooking time: 2 minutes - Preparation time: 5 minutes

method

1. Place cocoa powder and sugar in saucepan. Slowly stir in a little milk (a) to make a smooth paste. Stir in remaining milk.
2. Boil over a low heat, stirring all the time (b).
3. Carefully pour hot chocolate into mug (c). Place marshmallow on top.

....
Makes 1

ingredients

> **1 teaspoon cocoa powder**
> **1-2 teaspoons sugar, or according to taste**
> **1 cup/250 ml/8 fl oz cold milk**
> **1 marshmallow**

junior chef says

It is ideal for a winter day. If you wish to give it a special flavor, add a pinch of ground cinnamon.

a

b

c

yogurt
fruit whiz

■□□ | Cooking time: 0 minute - Preparation time: 5 minutes

ingredients

> **1 piece soft fruit of your choice such as a banana, peach, apricot, mango, or 125 g/4 oz strawberries or other berries of your choice**
> **2 ice cubes**
> **1 cup/200 g/6½ oz fruit-flavored yogurt of your choice**
> **1-2 tablespoons honey, or according to taste**

method

1. Remove stones or pits from fruit if you need to.
2. Peel fruit if you need to.
3. Place ice cubes in plastic food bag. Wrap in newspaper. Hit several times with hammer or rolling pin to crush.
4. Place fruit, crushed ice, yogurt and honey in food processor or blender. Process until thick and smooth. Pour into glass.

Makes 1

junior chef says

If fresh fruit is not available, this drink is just as good made with canned fruit. Remember to drain canned fruit well before using.

cheesy corn chips

■ □ □ | Cooking time: 7 minutes - Preparation time: 5 minutes

method

1. Preheat oven to 200°C/400°F/Gas 6.
2. Grate cheese (a). Set aside.
3. Cut bulb from spring onions. Remove outer leaves. Chop. Set aside.
4. Place corn chips in ovenproof dish. Sprinkle with cheese, spring onions (b) and paprika or chili powder.
5. Bake for 5 minutes or until cheese melts.

ingredients

> **60 g/2 oz tasty cheese (mature Cheddar)**
> **2 spring onions**
> **100 g/3¹/₂ oz packet corn chips**
> **pinch paprika or chili powder**

....
Serves 2

a

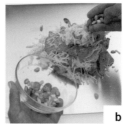

b

junior chef says
If you don't have corn chips, use home bread toasts instead.

old-fashioned
cheese on toast

■☐☐ | Cooking time: 5 minutes - Preparation time: 5 minutes

ingredients
> **2 slices bread**
> **2 tablespoons grated tasty cheese (mature Cheddar)**
> **pinch paprika or chili powder**

method
1. Preheat grill to hot.
2. Place bread under grill. Grill for 1-2 minutes or until golden.
3. Sprinkle untoasted side of bread with cheese and paprika or chili powder.
4. Grill for 2-3 minutes or until cheese melts.

....
Makes 2

junior chef says
For something different try topping bread with sliced tomato or spreading with chutney, relish or jam before sprinkling with cheese. If using jam replace paprika or chili powder with ground mixed spice.

flying saucers

■□□ | Cooking time: 5 minutes - Preparation time: 5 minutes

method

1. Preheat grill to high.
2. Cut ham or salami into strips. Set aside.
3. Cut muffin in half.
4. Spread each muffin half with tomato purée or tomato sauce.
5. Top with tomato slices. Sprinkle with ham or salami and cheese.
6. Place muffins under grill. Cook for 3-4 minutes or until cheese melts.

Makes 2

ingredients

> 1 slice ham or salami
> 1 wholemeal or plain muffin
> 1 tablespoon tomato purée or tomato sauce
> 2 slices tomato
> 2 tablespoons grated mozzarella cheese

junior chef says

See if there are any leftovers in the refrigerator you can use as a topping on your muffin. Always start by spreading your muffin with tomato purée or tomato sauce and finish by sprinkling with cheese.

eggs in a frame

■□□ | Cooking time: 8 minutes - Preparation time: 5 minutes

method

1. Using cookie cutter cut center out of bread slices (a).
2. Place butter in frying pan. Heat over a medium heat until butter melts and sizzles.
3. Place bread in pan. Cook for 1-2 minutes or until golden. Turn over (b).
4. Break an egg into cup or small jug. Carefully pour egg into hole in one slice of bread (c). Repeat with remaining egg and bread.
5. Place lid on pan. Cook for 4-5 minutes or until eggs are cooked as you like them.

ingredients

> **2 slices bread**
> **15 g/1/2 oz butter**
> **2 eggs**

....
Serves 2

junior chef says

Make this recipe using your favorite type of bread. My favorite bread is wholegrain.

a

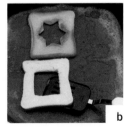

b

c

accordion
sandwich

■□□ I Cooking time: 15 minutes - Preparation time: 10 minutes

ingredients

> **6 slices tasty cheese (mature Cheddar)**
> **6 slices ham**
> **1 long French breadstick**
> **fruit chutney or mustard, according to taste**

method

1. Preheat oven to 220°C/425°F/Gas 7.
2. Line baking tray with nonstick baking paper.
3. Cut cheese slices and ham slices in half. Set aside.
4. Using serrated-edged knife, cut French breadstick into 12 even slices (a). Do not cut through base of loaf.
5. Spread one side of each cut with chutney or mustard (b).
6. Place a slice of cheese and a slice of ham in each cut.
7. Place loaf on baking tray. Bake for 10-15 minutes or until cheese just melts.

....
Serves 4

junior chef says

Accordion sandwich is delicious served with a big green salad (page 34).

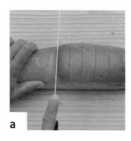

a

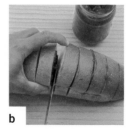

b

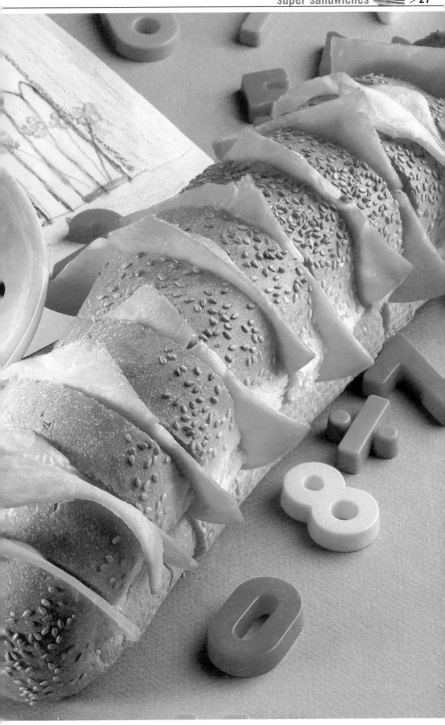

hero
sandwich

■□□ | Cooking time: 0 minute - Preparation time: 5 minutes

method

1. Cut French breadstick in half lengthwise. Set aside.
2. Place mayonnaise, mustard and yogurt in bowl. Mix.
3. Spread mayonnaise mixture over cut sides of breadstick. Set aside.
4. Place lettuce leaves on bottom half of breadstick. Top with ham, beef or turkey and salami.
5. Place tomatoes and cheese on top of meat. Top with other half of breadstick.
6. Tie breadstick at intervals with string. Cut into four.

....
Serves 4

ingredients

> 1 long French breadstick
> 4 tablespoons mayonnaise
> 1 tablespoon wholegrain mustard
> 2 tablespoons natural yogurt
> 6 large lettuce leaves
> 125 g/4 oz thinly sliced ham, roast beef or turkey
> 60 g/2 oz thinly sliced salami
> 2 thickly sliced tomatoes
> 4 slices tasty cheese (mature Cheddar)

junior chef says
To make the sandwich crunchier, melt the cheese over the bread before assembling.

american
hot dogs

■□□ | Cooking time: 5 minutes - Preparation time: 5 minutes

ingredients
> **4 long rolls**
> **butter**
> **water**
> **4 frankfurters**
> **ketchup, mild mustard or chutney**

method
1. Cut rolls in half lengthwise. Leave one side uncut. Spread lightly with butter. Set aside.
2. Three-quarters fill saucepan with water. Boil over a high heat.
3. Add frankfurters to saucepan. Boil for 5 minutes. Drain.
4. Place a frankfurter in each roll. Top with ketchup, mustard or chutney.

Makes 4

junior chef says
Serve hot dogs with a glass of juice or milk and a piece of fresh fruit and you'll have a complete meal.

world's
best hamburgers

■ □ □ | Cooking time: 10 minutes - Preparation time: 10 minutes

method

1. To make patties, place egg and ketchup in bowl. Whisk.
2. Place bread in food processor or blender. Process to make breadcrumbs.
3. Add breadcrumbs and mince to bowl with egg mixture. Add black pepper to taste. Mix. Shape beef mixture into 6 patties (a).
4. Place vegetable oil in frying pan. Heat over a medium heat until hot. Add patties to pan. Cook for 4-5 minutes (b). Turn over. Cook for 4-5 minutes.
5. Cut rolls in half. Cut each tomato into 6 slices. Set aside.
6. To assemble burgers, place a lettuce leaf on bottom half of each roll. Top with a patty, a slice of cheese (c), 2 tomato slices, some ketchup and top of roll.

ingredients

- > 1 tablespoon vegetable oil
- > 6 white or brown round rolls
- > 2 large tomatoes
- > 6 large lettuce leaves
- > 6 slices of your favorite cheese
- > 3 tablespoons ketchup

hamburger patties

- > 1 egg
- > 1 tablespoon ketchup
- > 2 slices stale bread
- > 500 g/1 lb lean beef mince
- > freshly ground black pepper

....
Makes 6

junior chef says

You might like to add some of the following to your hamburgers: beetroot slices, fried onion slices, a fried egg or a grilled bacon rasher.

a

b

c

a big green salad

■□□ | Cooking time: 0 minute - Preparation time: 10 minutes

ingredients

> **1 lettuce**
> **2 stalks celery**
> **1 tomato**
> **1/2 cucumber**
> **2 spring onions**

dressing

> **2 tablespoons olive oil**
> **1/4 cup/60 ml/3 fl oz lemon juice**
> **1/4 cup/60 ml/3 fl oz vinegar**
> **1/4 teaspoon dry mustard**
> **1/2 teaspoon sugar**
> **freshly ground black pepper**

method

1. Separate lettuce leaves. Wash in cold water. Drain in colander. Tear leaves into large pieces. Place in salad bowl.
2. Chop celery. Chop or slice tomato. Peel and slice cucumber. Cut bulbs from spring onions, remove outer leaves, chop. Add all ingredients to bowl.
3. To make dressing, place oil, lemon juice, vinegar, mustard, sugar and black pepper to taste in a screwtop jar. Place lid on jar. Shake well.
4. Pour dressing over salad. Using salad servers or two large spoons carefully toss salad.

Serves 4-6

junior chef says

Salads are great fun to make because you can add to them almost anything that you like. Try adding some of the following: sliced radishes, grated or cubed cheese, sliced raw mushrooms, sliced or grated raw carrots, chopped or sliced avocado, nuts like walnuts, almonds or peanuts and chopped fresh herbs like parsley, chives, mint and basil.

cheesy scalloped potatoes

■□□ | Cooking time: 80 minutes - Preparation time: 10 minutes

method

1. Preheat oven to 180°C/350°F/Gas 4.
2. Scrub potatoes under cold running water to remove all dirt, slice thinly (a). Peel onion, chop. Chop butter. Set aside.
3. Brush ovenproof dish with oil. Place a layer of potatoes in baking dish. Sprinkle with some onion (b) and black pepper. Top with a few pieces of butter. Repeat layers until all potato, onion and butter are used.
4. Place milk in saucepan. Stirring all the time, bring almost to boiling over a low heat.
5. Carefully pour milk over potato mixture (c).
6. Grate cheese. Sprinkle over potatoes.
7. Bake for 1-1¼ hours or until potatoes are tender.

ingredients

> 3 large potatoes
> 1 small onion
> 30 g/1 oz butter
> vegetable oil
> freshly ground black pepper
> 1¼ cups/315 ml/ 10 fl oz milk
> 60 g/2 oz tasty cheese (mature Cheddar)

....
Serves 4

junior chef says

If you like garlic, finely chop one or two cloves and use them instead of onion... or along with it!

a   b   c

stir-fry vegetables

■□□ I Cooking time: 20 minutes - Preparation time: 10 minutes

ingredients
> 1 clove garlic
> 1 onion
> 1 carrot
> 1 small head broccoli
> 2 stalks celery
> 1 red or green pepper
> 2 spring onions
> 1 teaspoon cornflour
> 1 tablespoon soy sauce
> 1/2 cup/125 ml/4 fl oz cold stock or water
> 2 tablespoons vegetable oil
> freshly ground black pepper

method
1. Crush garlic. Peel and slice onion. Peel carrot, slice diagonally. Cut thick stems from broccoli, separate broccoli into small flowerets. Slice celery diagonally (a). Set aside.
2. Remove stems and seeds from red or green pepper, slice (b). Cut bulbs from spring onions, remove outer leaves, slice diagonally into 5 cm/2 in lengths. Set aside.
3. Place cornflour, soy sauce and stock or water in small bowl. Mix. Set aside.
4. Heat wok or frying pan over a high heat until hot. Add oil, garlic and onion. Stir-fry for 2-3 minutes.
5. Add carrot. Stir-fry for 3-4 minutes.
6. Add broccoli. Stir-fry for 3-4 minutes.
7. Add celery and red or green pepper (c). Stir-fry for 2 minutes.
8. Add cornflour mixture. Cook, stirring all the time, for 2-3 minutes or until mixture boils and thickens.
9. Add spring onions and black pepper to taste. Toss. Serve immediately.

junior chef says
The secret when stir-frying is to have all the ingredients prepared before you start cooking.

Serves 4

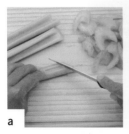

a

b

c

baked
jacket potatoes

■□□ | Cooking time: 1 hour - Preparation time: 10 minutes

method

1. Preheat oven to 200°C/400°F/Gas 6.
2. Scrub potatoes under cold running water to remove all dirt. Pierce skin of potatoes several times with fork (a).
3. Place potatoes on baking tray. Bake for 1 hour or until cooked.
4. Cut a cross in top of potatoes (b). Hold either end of each potato with clean cloth and push up (c). Set aside.
5. To make topping, cut bulb from spring onions. Remove outer leaves. Chop.
6. Top each cut potato with 1 tablespoon sour cream or yogurt. Sprinkle with 1 tablespoon cheese and some spring onions.

ingredients

> 4 medium or large potatoes –depending on how hungry you are and what else you will be having for your meal

traditional topping

> 2 spring onions
> 4 tablespoons sour cream or natural yogurt
> 4 tablespoons grated cheese

....
Makes 4

junior chef says

The beef mixture used in the tacos recipe (page 52) is a delicious and nutritious topping for baked potatoes.

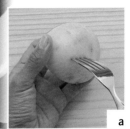

a

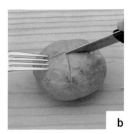

b

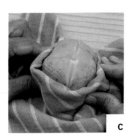

c

crazy soup

■□□ | Cooking time: 35 minutes - Preparation time: 10 minutes

ingredients

> **1 onion**
> **2 carrots**
> **2 sticks celery**
> **2 potatoes**
> **440 g/14 oz canned tomatoes**
> **2 tablespoons vegetable oil**
> **4 cups/1 litre/1³/4 pt water**
> **2 chicken or beef stock cubes**
> **125 g/4 oz pasta shapes**
> **freshly ground black pepper**

method

1. Peel and chop onion. Peel and slice carrots. Trim ends from celery sticks, slice. Set aside.
2. Scrub potatoes to remove dirt. Chop. Set aside.
3. Open can. Place tomatoes and juice in small bowl. Using scissors chop tomatoes.
4. Place oil in large saucepan. Heat over a medium heat for 3-4 minutes. Add onion. Cook, stirring, for 2-3 minutes.
5. Add carrots, celery and potatoes. Cook, stirring, for 4-5 minutes.
6. Add tomatoes, water and stock cubes. Boil, stirring, for 10 minutes.
7. Add pasta shapes. Stirring, cook for 10 minutes. Add black pepper to taste.
8. To serve, ladle soup into serving bowls.

....
Serves 6

junior chef says
To chop tomatoes with scissors, hold the scissors upright in bowl and chop.

macaroni
cheese

■□□ I Cooking time: 40 minutes - Preparation time: 10 minutes

method

1. Preheat oven to 200°C/400°F/Gas 6.
2. Grate cheese. Set aside.
3. Three-quarters fill large saucepan with water. Boil over a high heat. Add oil and macaroni. Boil for 10 minutes or until macaroni are cooked.
4. Meanwhile, to make sauce, place butter in medium saucepan. Heat over a medium heat until butter melts.
5. Remove from heat. Stir in flour. Return to heat. Cook, stirring, for 1 minute.
6. Remove from heat. Whisk in milk. Return to heat. Cook, stirring for 4-5 minutes or until sauce boils and thickens. Remove pan from heat.
7. Add black pepper to taste. Stir in half the grated cheese. Set aside.
8. Drain macaroni. Place in ovenproof dish. Pour sauce over. Sprinkle with remaining cheese. Sprinkle with paprika.
9. Bake for 20-25 minutes or until top is golden.

ingredients

> **125 g/4 oz tasty cheese (mature Cheddar)**
> **1 teaspoon vegetable oil**
> **250 g/8 oz macaroni**
> **30 g/1 oz butter**
> **3 tablespoons flour**
> **2 cups/500 ml/16 fl oz milk**
> **freshly ground black pepper**
> **paprika**

....
Serves 4

junior chef says

Another very traditional version consists in mixing pasta with cooked broccoli, then adding the sauce and putting it into the oven.

real pizza

■ □ □ | Cooking time: 20 minutes - Preparation time: 5 minutes

method

1. Preheat oven to 220°C/425°F/Gas 7.
2. Grate cheese. Set aside.
3. Prepare your choice of toppings –you can use just one or any combination that you like (a). Set aside.
4. Place pizza base on baking tray. Spread with tomato paste (b). Sprinkle with dried herbs (if you wish).
5. Add toppings. Sprinkle with cheese (c). Bake for 20 minutes or until base is cooked.

Serves 4

ingredients

> 90 g/3 oz mozzarella cheese
> 1 purchased pizza base
> 3 tablespoons tomato paste (purée)
> 1/2 teaspoon mixed dried herbs (if you like them)

toppings to choose

> sliced salami
> chopped ham
> tomato slices
> chopped or sliced onion
> chopped green or red pepper
> sliced or chopped green or black olives
> pineapple pieces
> sliced mushrooms
> anchovy fillets

junior chef says

Pizza is great fun to make because you can top it with whatever you like. It is also fun to arrange the food in patterns, pictures or faces.

a

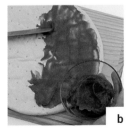
b

c

mystery pie

■□□ | Cooking time: 50 minutes - Preparation time: 10 minutes

method

1. Preheat oven to 180°C/350°F/Gas 4.
2. Place eggs, milk and flour in large bowl. Whisk (a).
3. Open can. Drain salmon or tuna. Place in small bowl. Using fork break up. Add to egg mixture.
4. Chop red or green pepper. Grate cheese. Add both to egg mixture. Mix.
5. Add parsley (b) and black pepper to taste to egg mixture. Mix.
6. Lightly brush flan dish with vegetable oil. Pour in egg mixture (c). Bake for 45-50 minutes or until pie is firm. Stand for 5 minutes. Cut into wedges.

....
Serves 6

ingredients

> 4 eggs
> 2 cups/500 ml/16 fl oz milk
> 3/4 cup/125 g/4 oz wholemeal flour
> 100 g/3 1/2 oz canned salmon or tuna
> 1/2 red or green pepper
> 125 g/4 oz tasty cheese (mature Cheddar)
> 2 tablespoons chopped fresh parsley
> freshly ground black pepper
> 1 tablespoon vegetable oil

junior chef says

This is called "mystery pie" because as it cooks a crust forms on the bottom of it.

a

b

c

melting meatballs

■□□ I Cooking time: 30 minutes - Preparation time: 10 minutes

ingredients

> **¼ cup/60 ml/2 fl oz beef stock**
> **2 eggs**
> **1 teaspoon mixed dried herbs**
> **1 teaspoon Worcestershire sauce**
> **4 slices stale wholemeal bread**
> **1 onion**
> **1 carrot**
> **500 g/1 lb lean beef mince**
> **freshly ground black pepper**
> **90 g/3 oz tasty cheese**
> **vegetable oil**
> **1 egg**
> **1 cup/125 g/4 oz dried breadcrumbs**
> **flour**

method

1. Preheat oven to 180°C/350°F/Gas 4.
2. Place stock, eggs, herbs and Worcestershire sauce in a large bowl; whisk.
3. Process bread slices, add to bowl. Peel and grate onion and carrot, add to bowl. Add beef mince and black pepper to taste, mix. Set aside.
4. Cut cheese into twelve 1 cm/¾ in cubes. Divide meat mixture into twelve equal portions. Mold one portion of meat mixture around each cube of cheese. Set aside.
5. Lightly brush baking dish with vegetable oil. Set aside.
6. Whisk egg in small bowl. Place breadcrumbs on plate. Place flour on other plate.
7. Roll each meatball in flour. Dip in egg. Roll in breadcrumbs. Place in baking dish.
8. Bake for 25-30 minutes or until cooked.

....
Serves 4

junior chef says

To make stock, place 1 beef stock cube and ¼ cup/60 ml/2 fl oz hot water in a bowl, mix, cool.

tasty tacos

■□□ | Cooking time: 20 minutes - Preparation time: 10 minutes

method

1. Preheat oven to 180°C/350°F/Gas 4.
2. Peel and chop onion. Crush garlic. Set aside.
3. Place oil in frying pan. Heat over a medium heat until hot. Add onion and garlic. Cook, stirring, for 5-6 minutes.
4. Add beef. Cook, stirring, for 5 minutes (a).
5. Stir in taco seasoning mix, water (b) and tomato sauce. Cook, stirring, for 5 minutes.
6. Place taco shells on baking tray. Heat in oven for 5 minutes.
7. Roll lettuce leaves, cut into strips. Cut tomatoes into small pieces. Set aside.
8. Spoon beef mixture into taco shells (c). Top with lettuce, tomato and cheese.

....
Serves 4

ingredients

> **1 large onion**
> **2 cloves garlic (if you like it)**
> **1 tablespoon vegetable oil**
> **500 g/1 lb lean beef mince**
> **30 g/1 oz taco seasoning mix**
> **1/2 cup/125 ml/4 fl oz water**
> **3 tablespoons tomato sauce**
> **8 taco shells**
> **4 large lettuce leaves**
> **2 tomatoes**
> **4 tablespoons grated tasty cheese (mature Cheddar)**

junior chef says

For a complete meal serve tacos with a big green salad (page 34).

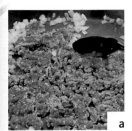
a

b

c

apple
crumble

■□□ | Cooking time: 35 minutes - Preparation time: 10 minutes

ingredients

> **3 apples**

crumble topping

> **3/4 cup/125 g/4 oz brown sugar**
> **1/2 cup/60 g/2 oz flour**
> **3/4 cup/75 g/2 1/2 oz rolled oats**
> **60 g/2 oz butter**

method

1. Preheat oven to 180°C/350°F/Gas 4.
2. Cut apples into quarters. Cut out cores. Peel. Slice thinly.
3. Place apple slices in ovenproof dish.
4. To make topping, place sugar, flour and rolled oats in bowl. Chop butter into pieces. Add to bowl.
5. Using your fingers mix in butter until mixture is crumbly.
6. Sprinkle topping over apples. Bake for 35 minutes.

....

Serves 6

junior chef says

Eat it lukewarm, served with lightly whipped cream or vanilla ice-cream, and you will really enjoy it!

ice cream
sandwiches

■□□ | Cooking time: 0 minute - Preparation time: 5 minutes

method

1. Spread bottom of one biscuit with ice cream.
2. Top with second biscuit.
3. Place on freezerproof dish. Freeze until ice cream is hard.

ingredients

> **2 biscuits**
> **1 spoonful soft ice cream**

....
Makes 1

junior chef says

Try these cosmic combos.
Chocolate chip biscuits with chocolate ice cream.
Chocolate chip biscuits with vanilla ice cream.
Gingernuts with vanilla ice cream.
Best of all is your favorite biscuit teamed with your favorite ice cream.

face biscuits

■□□ | Cooking time: 20 minutes - Preparation time: 25 minutes

ingredients

> **185 g/6 oz soft butter**
> **3/4 cup/185 g/6 oz sugar**
> **1 egg**
> **1/4 teaspoon vanilla essence**
> **13/4 cups/220 g/7 oz flour**

vanilla icing

> **11/2 cup/220 g/7 oz icing sugar**
> **60 g/2 oz butter, softened**
> **2 tablespoons boiling water**
> **1/4 teaspoon vanilla essence**
> **food colorings of your choice**
> **selection of sweets**

method

1. Beat butter and sugar in bowl until light and creamy. Add egg and vanilla essence, beat. Sift flour into mixture. Mix.
2. Turn dough onto a lightly floured surface. Knead for 3-4 minutes or until dough is smooth.
3. Divide dough into two portions. Roll each portion into a log (a). Wrap in plastic food wrap. Refrigerate for 3-4 hours.
4. Cut dough logs into 5 mm/1/4 in slices (b). Place on lined baking tray. Bake at 180°C/350°F/Gas 4 for 15-18 minutes or until biscuits are lightly browned. Place on wire rack to cool.
5. To make icing, sift icing sugar into a bowl. Add butter and boiling water, mix. Beat in vanilla essence.
6. Divide icing between small bowls. Add a few drops of food coloring to each portion of icing. Mix. Spread biscuits with icing (c). Decorate with sweets to make funny faces (d).

....
Makes 30

junior chef says

If you wish to make chocolate biscuits, add 1 tablespoon cocoa powder to flour.

a

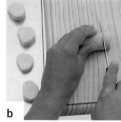

b

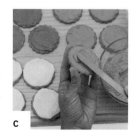

c

butterfly cakes

■■□ | Cooking time: 15 minutes - Preparation time: 25 minutes

method

1. Preheat oven to 200°C/400°F/Gas 6.
2. Place water and butter in saucepan. Heat over a low heat until butter melts. Cool slightly.
3. Place eggs in bowl, whisk. Sift flour into bowl. Add sugar, milk and butter. Mix.
4. Spoon batter evenly into patty cake tins. Bake for 10-12 minutes or until a skewer inserted into center of a cake comes out clean.
5. Stand 5 minutes. Remove from tins. Place on wire rack to cool.
6. Cut jelly snakes into pieces. Set aside. Place cream in a bowl, whip until soft peaks form. Set aside.
7. Cut top from each cake to form a shallow hole (a). Set aside.
8. Place a little jam in each cake. Top with whipped cream (b).
9. Cut top of each cake in half (c). Place straight sides down on cream. Place a piece of jelly snake in center.
10. Place icing sugar in sifter or sieve. Sift over top of cakes.

Makes 24

ingredients

> 2 teaspoons water
> 60 g/2 oz butter
> 2 eggs
> 1¹/2 cups/185 g/6 oz self-raising flour
> 1/2 cup/100 g/3¹/2 oz caster sugar
> 1/2 cup/125 ml/4 fl oz milk

topping

> 12 jelly snakes
> 1 cup/250 ml/8 fl oz cream
> 4 tablespoons of your favorite jam
> icing sugar

junior chef says

If you want to make chocolate-flavored cakes, dissolve 2 teaspoons cocoa powder in 2 teaspoons hot water and use instead of the water.

a

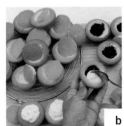

b

c

apricot
spice muffins

■□□ | Cooking time: 25 minutes - Preparation time: 10 minutes

method

1. Preheat oven to 180°C/350°F/Gas 4. Lightly brush muffin tins with vegetable oil (a).
2. Place self-raising flour, wholemeal self-raising flour and mixed spice in sifter or sieve. Sift into large bowl. Tip any husks remaining in sifter or sieve into bowl. Use scissors to cut apricots into small pieces. Add apricots to flour mixture. Set aside.
3. Place butter in saucepan. Heat over a low heat until butter melts. Pour butter into small bowl. Add lemon juice, lemon rind, sugar and egg. Whisk.
4. Pour half the butter mixture into flour mixture (b), mix. Pour in half the milk, mix. Repeat to use all the butter mixture and milk.
5. Spoon mixture into muffin tins (c). Bake for 20-25 minutes or until a skewer inserted into the center of a muffin comes out clean.
6. Stand muffins in tins for 5 minutes. Turn onto wire rack. Cool.

....
Makes 12

ingredients

> **vegetable oil for brushing tins**
> **1¹/4 cups/155 g/5 oz self-raising flour**
> **3/4 cup/100 g/3¹/2 oz wholemeal self-raising flour**
> **1 teaspoon ground mixed spice**
> **155 g/5 oz dried apricots**
> **90 g/3 oz butter**
> **1 tablespoon lemon juice**
> **1 tablespoon grated lemon rind**
> **1/3 cup/60 g/2 oz brown sugar**
> **1 egg**
> **1/2 cup/125 ml/4 fl oz milk**

junior chef says

I like to make these muffins at the weekend so that we have instant snack food during the week.

a

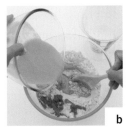
b

c

index